For my community of Vermont College
of Fine Arts picture book writers
—J. K.

For my awesome parents
—A. B.

BEACH LANE BOOKS • An imprint of Simon & Schuster Children's Publishing Division • 1230 Avenue of the Americas, New York, New York 10020 • Text copyright © 2018 by Jane Kurtz • Illustrations copyright © 2018 by Allison Black • All rights reserved, including the right of reproduction in whole or in part in any form. • BEACH LANE BOOKS is a trademark of Simon & Schuster, Inc. • For information about special discounts for bulk purchases, please contact Simon & Schuster Special Sales at 1-866-506-1949 or business@simonandschuster.com. • The Simon & Schuster Speakers Bureau can bring authors to your live event. For more information or to book an event, contact the Simon & Schuster Speakers Bureau at 1-866-248-3049 or visit our website at www.simonspeakers.com. • Book design by Lauren Rille • The text for this book was set in Rockwell. • Manufactured in China • 0418 SCP • First Edition • 10 9 8 7 6 5 4 3 2 1 • CIP data for this book is available from the Library of Congress. • ISBN 978-1-4814-7986-8 • ISBN 978-1-4814-7987-5 (eBook)

WHAT THEY DO
WITH ALL THAT

written by
Jane Kurtz

illustrated by
Allison Black

Beach Lane Books • New York London Toronto Sydney New Delhi

At zoo after zoo
the animals chew.
And then . . .

they poo!

Poo is made of mostly water but also bacteria and bits of undigested food. Animal poo goes by a lot of different names, including manure, scat, droppings, dung, castings, and guano.

Giraffe poop looks like marbles as it drops a long, long way.

A giraffe has four stomachs, so it digests its food very efficiently. That means a giraffe needs to eat a lot less than most herbivores, which is why its droppings are so small.

Panda poo is full of bamboo.
Pandas eat and poop all day.

Pandas digest only 17% of the bamboo they eat, and the leaves and stems pass through their systems very quickly, so panda poop looks like a green mass of partly digested bamboo—and it doesn't stink!

A hippo sprays a shower
with its flipping, flapping tail.

Hippos use dung showering to mark their territories and warn off predators. They shoot their dung out while flapping their tails to spray it around.

To weigh a day of an elephant's poo, you need a sturdy scale.

An elephant can eat 300 pounds of leaves and grasses a day and then dump 165 pounds of poo. (To help you think about that, a football weighs about a pound.)

Rhinos can communicate
through piles and piles of scat.

HELLO

BOB WAS HERE

Each rhino's poop has its own unique smell. Rhinos smell dung
to gather information about one another.

A lion sometimes buries poo— like any other cat.

Cats big and little often bury their poop so it won't be detected by enemies. But sometimes lions and tigers leave poop unburied as a warning that this is their territory.

Sloths creep down from trees to poop,
but only once a week.

Why do sloths spend so much energy leaving the protection
of trees to poop on the ground? It's a mystery scientists are
trying to solve.

A penguin shoots its poo out
in a fishy-smelling streak.

Penguins don't have teeth, so, as one zookeeper says, "fish go
through them fairly rapidly." Scientists have studied the force it
takes for a penguin to shoot its bright-white fishy guano so far.

A wombat's poo is cube-shaped,
so it isn't very roly.

Wombats are highly territorial. They each deposit 80–100 droppings every evening as signposts to say "I'm here." (It helps to have a square signpost that doesn't roll away.)

Some snakes poop only once a year.
They digest their food sloooow-ly.

One study showed that it took a python 5½ days to digest a rat. Because their bodies are so efficient, snakes poop less often than almost any other animal.

Hyenas crunch up lots of bones.
That's why their poop is white.

The calcium in bones is what makes dried hyena poop white—and why hyena poop can easily turn into a fossil.

Bat poop has undigested bugs—bats poop all day and night.

Bats turn right side up to do their poo so they don't poop on themselves. A bat can eat up to 1,200 mosquitoes in an hour. Many bats also eat insects with shiny outer coverings that don't get digested, which makes the bats' poop sparkly!

So what do zoos **do**

with all of that **poo**?

They sweep it

and hose it

and toss it each day.

A lot goes in dumpsters
to be trucked away.

A zoo might have to deal with more than 5,000 pounds of poop each day. Keeping it around would make zoos pretty smelly, so some of them pay thousands of dollars a year to send it off in trucks to landfills.

They send some to vets
and to scientists, too.

Then zoo poop is studied to help out the zoo.

Doctors and vets study poop to see how well an animal is digesting its food and to spot health problems. Some zoos are experimenting with using poop to produce bio-gas that can power vehicles or buildings like a zoo hospital.

They pile some in towers
and toss it with rakes.

It soon will be compost
for gardeners to take.

Compost—made from herbivore poop mixed with food waste
and grass clippings—improves soil and helps plants grow.
Zoos sell or give away compost using creative names like Zoo
Manoo, Zoo Doo, and Pachy Poo. Carnivore poo can be
spread around yards to keep deer from eating plants and trees.

First, worms like to munch it.
Their poop is so teeny!

Then worm poop plus zoo poop grows perfect zoo-chini!

Worms are an important part of the zoo-poo composting process. They can eat hundreds of pounds of organic matter every week! Woodland Park Zoo in Seattle sells Worm Doo, made from Zoo Doo compost and zoo coffee grounds. The zoo says, "It's been pooped once by exotic herbivores and pooped again by compost-loving worms."

They even make paper from elephant poo.

Elephant poo comes out with so much plant fiber that a machine can wash the poo and pull out the fiber, which can then be used to make paper and cards.

Zoo-poo paper's pretty,
not smelly. It's true!

DUCK!

That monkey at the zoo . . .

just threw
its poo at **you!**

Many primates throw poo. Scientists discovered that chimpanzees who throw the most poo and hit their target the most often are the smartest and most sociable, which suggests that throwing is a form of communication and self-expression—and maybe a step toward using tools.